LET'S-READ-AND-FIND-OUT SCIENCE®

What Lives in a Shell?

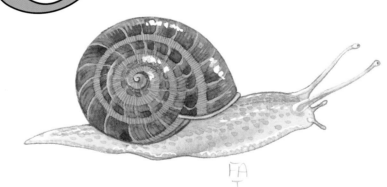

by Kathleen Weidner Zoehfeld • illustrated by Helen K. Davie

HarperCollinsPublishers

The *Let's-Read-and-Find-Out Science* book series was originated by Dr. Franklyn M. Branley, Astronomer Emeritus and former Chairman of the American Museum–Hayden Planetarium, and was formerly co-edited by him and Dr. Roma Gans, Professor Emeritus of Childhood Education, Teachers College, Columbia University. Text and illustrations for each book in the series are checked for accuracy by an expert in the relevant field. For a complete catalog of Let's-Read-and-Find-Out Science books, write to HarperCollins Children's Books, 10 East 53rd Street, New York, NY 10022.

WHAT LIVES IN A SHELL?

Library of Congress Cataloging-in-Publication Data
Zoehfeld, Kathleen Weidner.
   What lives in a shell? / by Kathleen Weidner Zoehfeld ; illustrated by Helen K. Davie.
      p.   cm. — (Let's-read-and-find-out science. Stage 1)
   Summary: Describes such animals as snails, turtles, and crabs, which live in shells and use these coverings as protection.
   ISBN 0-06-022998-5. — ISBN 0-06-022999-3 (lib. bdg.) — ISBN 0-06-445124-0 (pbk.)
   1. Body covering (Anatomy)—Juvenile literature. 2. Shells—Juvenile literature. [1. Shells. 2. Body covering (Anatomy). 3. Animal defenses.] I. Davie, Helen, ill. II. Title. III. Series.
QL941.Z64   1994   93-12428
591.4'71—dc20   CIP
                                                           AC

Typography by Elynn Cohen
1 2 3 4 5 6 7 8 9 10 ❖
First Edition

What Lives in a Shell?

Do you know what this is?

It is as hard as a stone. But it is not a stone.
It is smooth, like glass. But it is not glass.
It is hollow inside, like a cup. But it is not a cup.
It is a shell. An animal made it. The shell was
the animal's home.

You live in a house or in an apartment building.
That is your home. Your home keeps you safe and warm.

Lots of animals have homes.
Birds build nests.

Ants make tunnels underground.

A bear likes to live in a cave.

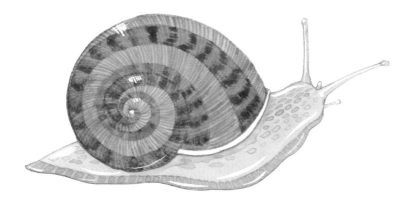

Here is the animal that lives in this kind of shell. It is a land snail.

A land snail is born with a tiny shell. As long as the snail lives, it keeps on growing.

As the snail grows, its shell grows with it. The shell keeps the snail safe.

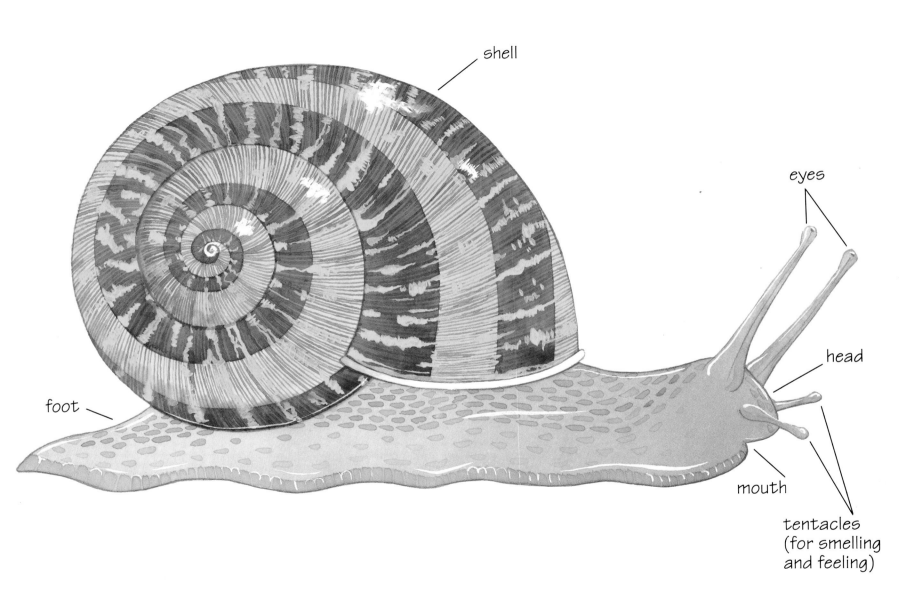

shell

eyes

head

foot

mouth

tentacles
(for smelling
and feeling)

9

You can go in and out of your home. You can run
to the playground. You can wait outside for the bus.

A snail never leaves its home. It takes its home with it wherever it goes.

The snail pokes its soft
head and its one big foot
out of the opening in its
shell. It uses its foot to
inch along. A snail is slow.

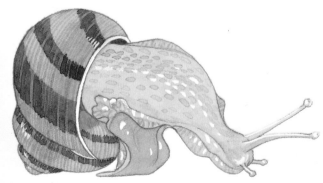

Birds like to eat snails. When a bird or other enemy comes around, a snail cannot run away. It pulls its head and foot inside its shell and closes the door. The snail is safe.

Other kinds of animals live in shells, too.
Shells come in many shapes, colors, and sizes.
Turtles live in shells. A turtle's shell can be
bumpy or smooth. Most are rounded on top and
flat on the belly.

Baby turtles have little shells. As the babies grow bigger, their shells grow bigger.

A turtle has four legs. It pokes its legs, head, and tail through the openings in its shell. Even though it has four legs, a turtle is slow.

Have you ever had a turtle race?

If a frog and a turtle were in a race, who do you think would win?

What about a cat and a turtle?

If a turtle sees a cat, it may be frightened. It may think the cat wants to eat it.

A turtle cannot run as fast as a cat. The turtle pulls its head and legs and tail into its shell. The cat pats the turtle with its paw. The turtle won't come out. It is safe in its shell home.

When you go to the seashore, you can find
many different kinds of shells.

You may see a crab walking on the sand. A crab
has ten legs. On its front legs are two claws. A
hard shell covers its claws and the rest of its body.

A crab's shell fits it like a suit of armor. The armor helps keep the crab safe from enemies.

But just as you outgrow your favorite shirt, a crab outgrows its shell. When it gets too tight, the crab pulls itself out. Underneath is a new shell.

You may find snails buried in the sand. Some of them do not look much like the land snails.

Whelks and conchs are types of snails that are found only by the sea. Here are some different kinds of sea-snail shells.

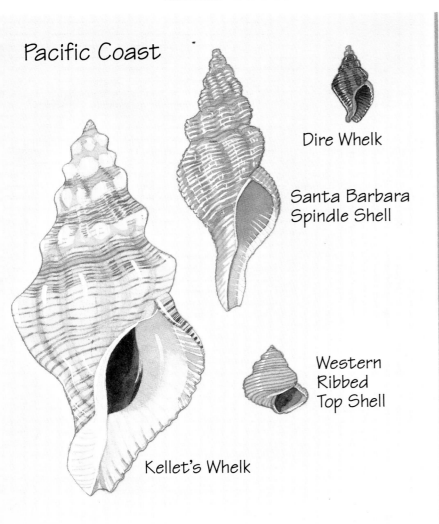

Pacific Coast

Dire Whelk

Santa Barbara Spindle Shell

Western Ribbed Top Shell

Kellet's Whelk

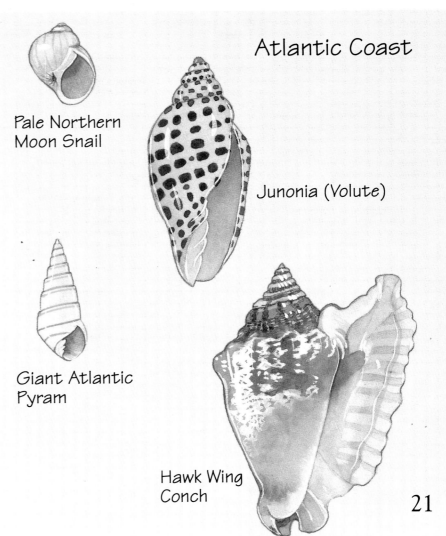

Atlantic Coast

Pale Northern Moon Snail

Junonia (Volute)

Giant Atlantic Pyram

Hawk Wing Conch

21

Have you ever seen a snail shell walking along on crab legs?

A hermit crab has hard claws in front, but the back end of its body has a soft shell. Its shell is too soft to keep it safe from enemies.

A hermit crab lives in an empty snail shell.

After a while the hermit crab grows too big for his shell. So he looks for a bigger one. Some are too big. Some are too small. Finally he finds one he likes. He throws away the old shell and crawls into the new one.

Now the new shell is his home. The snail shell helps keep him safe.

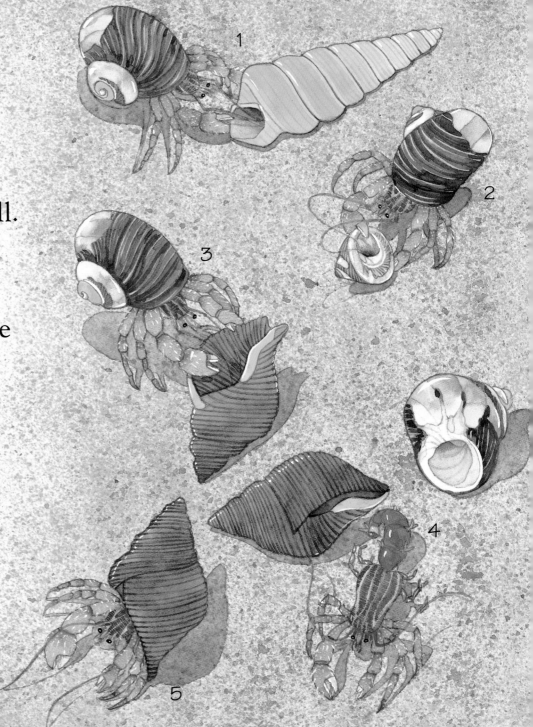

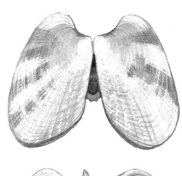

clam shell
outside

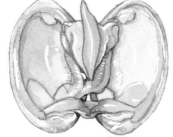

clam shell
inside

clam shell
hinge

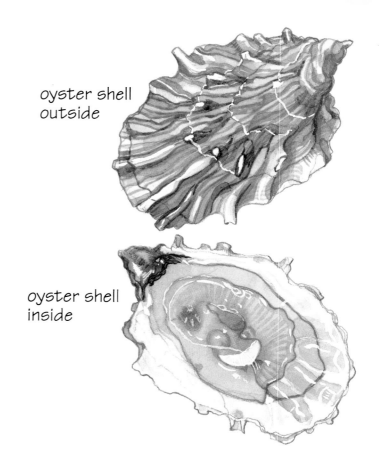

oyster shell
outside

oyster shell
inside

You can look for clam and oyster shells at the
beach, too. Clams and oysters are animals.

They have no legs. They do not have heads or
tails. Their bodies are soft. But they are animals.

Clams and oysters grow two hard shells. The top shell and bottom shell look almost alike. The two shells are connected by a hinge. Scallops also have two shells. Here are some different kinds of scallop shells.

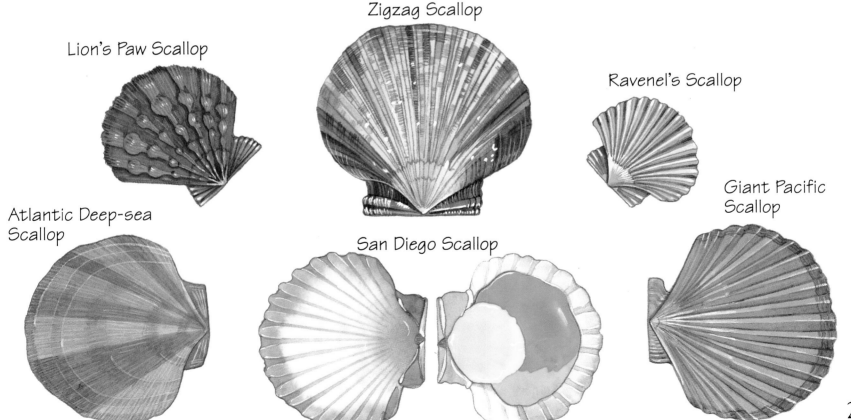

Lion's Paw Scallop

Zigzag Scallop

Ravenel's Scallop

Giant Pacific Scallop

Atlantic Deep-sea Scallop

San Diego Scallop

Most clams and oysters hardly move at all. They open up their shells to take in food and water. They close their shells tightly when enemies are around.

Some scallops can swim. A scallop does not swim like a fish, though. First it opens its two shells. Then it snaps them together quickly. This gets the scallop where it wants to go.

When you find a shell, carefully look inside.
It will probably be empty. If a shell is empty, it
may mean the animal has died. Or, it has outgrown
the shell and left it behind.

If the animal is at home, you can watch it for a
while. See if you can tell how it eats. How does it
move? What does it do when it feels frightened?

When you go, leave the animal where you found it. Animals are happiest in their natural surroundings. If a shell is empty, you can take it home with you.*

30

*If you are looking at shells in a state or national park, be sure to ask a ranger or game warden before you take any shells from the park.

31

Try to find as many different kinds of shells as you can. Whether the shells you find are big or small, plain or fancy—remember, a shell is someone's home.